THE BORDER

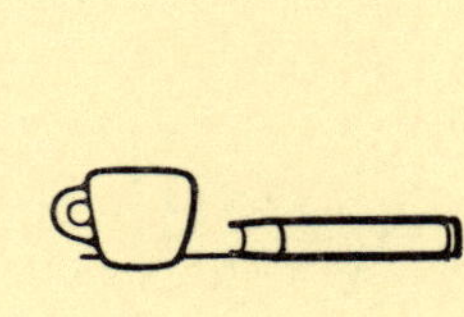

THE BORDER, A PLAY

The dark quiet ocean along the sandy shores of Veracruz,
where the exhausted Mediterranean flings itself on the beach
with a flash of scales, like a suicidal fish. . .

False hidalgos stripped to the waist conduct idle and
fractious dialogues under the moonlit palms, stopping
now and then to duel with knives; bodies flop to the sand. . .

Smoke partially obscures a vast bridge of timbers, from
beneath which a group of vagrants emerges to put on a
show for the rich—The Beggar's Opera. . .

A local pimp plays a highwayman in dirty scarlet coat
and muddied boots, daubing his lips now and then from an
opium cache kept in a wooden cigarette box. . .

Avarice and treachery, Gay seems to tell us in his play,
are not inbred but handed down from class to class
much as diseased legacies that infect history *in perpetuum*. . .

Brandy-swilling junior officers like characters out of
an Edwardian farce step forward to meet the sleazy,
bullet-headed opportunists who are leading the uprising. . .

Watching, we are sensitive to the smallest eddies and
currents of emotion, the equivocations of the sickly helots,
the muddy threats of the lords of gibbet and blade. . .

The songs intermingled with the drama create disjunct
time shifts that completely obscure the sense of the
text, a confusion increased by the appearance of the musicians. . .

They are a band of sawed-off natives armed with clarinet,
guitar, concertina and violins, instruments they wield more like
weapons, bickering even as they play, and sometimes attacking the audience. . .

There is a hazy neon image blinking on and off above the
stage: "Frontier. . . Frontier. . . Frontier," beyond which we just
make out the vague, dissolving image of a suspension bridge. . .

Its elegant span arches into an unknown of
which we can perceive only slight hints, like the wind
that whistles constantly in the brown-gray obscurity. . .

Off to the left a new group of musicians approaches
cautiously, midget-ruffians in severe dark suits, toting instrument-cases,
clutching the guardrails, chattering among themselves. . .

Shrill and inexplicable noises occasionally rise
from the empty eyesockets of these dilapidated mummies
who, we discover, are only "pretending" to be musicians. . .

Actually they are demented rag dolls without brains
whose schizophrenic jerking movements, we understand,
are controlled from somewhere offstage. . .

The absent *metteur-en-scene* is, we sense, also a diabolical
menteur-en-scene who wishes only to deceive
us with enigmas and illusions of manipulated space. . .

The lighting effects are mechanically conceived attempts
to make us uneasy, to split our personalities
and confuse us, in which they are completely successful. . .

Wind and fog machines, revved up full blast,
make the single gas footlight at the front of the stage
seem inexpressibly hopeless since it illuminates nothing. . .

But now an Indian summer glow begins to descend from
the false ceiling, creating an amazing likeness of the
valley of the St. Lawrence in October. . .

Six thousand men in 350 boats, forming a procession
five miles long, slide down the great river from
the left of the stage toward the right. . .

As the flotilla approaches center stage we gradually
realize that the captain is either drunk or badly reduced by
opium: he teeters precariously from the bow of the primary boat. . .

The men of the riverborne party are groaning terribly and clutching
their bellies, warning the audience to stand back: they are
suffering from a virulent form of amœbic dysentery. . .

From behind large clumps of bushes at stage right, the boats are fired
on by war parties of Indian stragglers, old hoboes
and red-satin vamps in Dracula sweatshirts. . .

The flotilla slows and twists agonizingly around
every channel as the river takes a new and more
complicated, intricate shape with winter coming on. . .

There is a sense of desolation, an Arctic chill
in the air and an unnerving desperation about the
landscape that tells us: we are crossing the border. . .

THE BORDER · A MOVIE

The bedchamber of a dying courtesan in Paris . . . a grim music
		struggles on damaged wings
through the emotion-charged air . . . fitful breathing . . . her
		townhouse in the hands of auctioneers . . .
there is no escape except through transformation . . . "one must . . . "
"*il faut qu'on . . .* " she hesitates, then gasps, "mutate or die!" . . .
		a last
bilingual exclamation turns into a bright pink flower of blood upon
her fever blanched lips . . . she swoons . . . the future is now . . .
		but that
is the same as never . . . she staggers from her bed, arms clutching
		at nothing,
and begins to croak out the fatal opening chords of what we know to be
her final aria . . . the audience, amused, untroubled, nods . . .
they are numb to her pain . . . they have seen *La Traviata*
		many times . . .

A vessel suddenly eludes the surgeon's hand and slips away,
like a freshwater fish not quite landed, into the soft folds of
		the brain . . .
as from an atomizer, blood sprays out over the surgical field in
		a fine mist . . .
"Don't stop the dance," her soul cries out wordlessly, "this may be
		my last chance . . ."

The woman inhabits a dimly lit flat filled with paintings
for which, years ago, she may have been the model . . . they exude
    a pale, silky light
that masks their subject's expression even as it defines her features . . .
a window opens out on an ambiguous landscape

which looks like it might have been created by the same painter
(now turned set designer) whose work covers the walls . . .
from the left, the iridescent glow of the sea glancing
off the white coral of an archipelago lined with palm trees
moves across the screen . . . the room gradually acquires a
        ghostly brightness
in subdued luminosities such as a prism might filter from the moon . . .
the woman sits at a table with folded hands, humming to herself . . .
night slowly falls . . . time, here, means nothing . . . outside,
        the workers' settlement
comes to life . . . the noisy promiscuity of company beer halls
provides mindless refuge from toil, as well as a thick local brew,
made from maize and sorghum, excessively fermented . . . further
up the broad main avenue of this colonial town we see luxury hotels
in whose uncommunicative bars sweating gentlemen in neckties
distractedly toss suction tip darts at images on television . . .
there is desultory wagering on prospective assassinations
        or executions . . .
the woman has no wish to join them . . . she remains alone,
as if in waiting for someone to arrive . . . some days have passed
since she herself appeared, tired and dusty, at the outskirts of town
in a Land Rover she'd maneuvered over endless dirt roads, under
        immense gunmetal skies,
stopping at the Chicken Shack Beer Lounge . . . where, to her
        relieved surprise,
an old man had greeted her with the double union handshake,
        thumbs to the sky . . .
this information is delivered to us in a series of montage-like flashbacks . . .

Pan to: a dark, narrow alley in the old quarter (subtitle reveals)
of Peking . . . stone pavement . . . patches of bare wall gleam like metal
in a steady drizzle . . . follow the multilingual signs . . . turn right
at the third corner and step through a low orange door . . . easy
        does it . . .
you enter a large auditorium . . . ceiling, walls and curving rows
        of high-backed
seats are draped with a pale, grayish-beige cloth . . . on which
beads of moisture seem to form constantly, as if by condensation . . .
or are they specks of paint? . . . on proscenium arch and rear columns,
        sculptural forms,
of gray and bloated plaster, loom in swollen caricature
of some 18th century ornamental grotto, like Pope's Folly
at Twickenham, with its glass, shells and agates laboriously clustered
upon walls and roof of a subterranean passage spanning the Thames . . .
the sense of sub-fluvial incrustation also reminds one of life
on board an antique submarine . . . somewhat more claustrophobic
than comfortable . . . still, minor anxieties and inconveniences aside,
one major question remains: why have we come and how did
        we get here? . . .
no one knows . . . ahead, in a long gallery that begins with the stage,
outdoor light peeks through . . . extravagant roofs emerge,
outlined against a hazy sky . . . silent ushers in silk tunics
pass through the audience, distributing strange runic books . . .
the writing is unclear but seems to concern decay, rebellion and war . . .
abruptly the lights go dim and a single actress, in shimmering
        brocade robes,

walks to the center of the stage and stands there stiffly, preparing
	to address us . . .
she opens her mouth to speak, but despite ourselves, we in the audience
drown out her words, howling and baying like a pack of
	spellbound mongrels . . .

What kind of witch or siren would make dogs out of men? is reality
	merely a droll joke?
The surgeon scrapes and teases his way around her brain stem
with exquisite care . . . moving millimeter by anxious millimeter
	into a region where
you don't ever pull too hard on anything . . . it just might be attached
	to the soul . . .

After crossing the central Himalayas in six days, she encounters
an even more menacing barrier, the Zaskar Range . . . *pays du monstre* . . .
and 50 miles beyond that . . . beyond obstacles almost mythically arduous . . .
yet another sheer mountain face, rising nearly vertical,
capped by a tremendous pyramid of snow and black granite
on which is emblazoned an ancient swastika over 300 yards
	in diameter . . .
this is Mt. Kailas, legendary primeval hub of the universe . . .
	and beneath its base
of scree and talus there opens out like a jewel dropped from heaven
the cool, still, iceslick-glinting, turquoise-sapphire-gleaming surface
of Lake Manasarovar . . . the sacred pool and shrine of deities
so archaic their names are now lost . . . with a high diver's expectant poise
she approaches the edge of a pier-like rock, shapes her arms into a sharp V
whose point touches space exactly a foot above her head,

and then, uncoiling like a perfect spring, plunges in a gliding arc
down toward the for-centuries-unvisited depths . . . the director
    raises his
right hand . . . the motor-drive camera, with its Swiss zoom lenses,

dollies in to capture a close-up of her entry into the water . . .
        at exactly that
moment a sudden cloud mass looms up over the mountain, blocking
        out the sun
completely . . . the entire tableau is obscured in fog and swirling mists . . .
when, a few seconds later, the air clears again, the diver is
        no longer visible . . .

. . . coming back up . . . swimming blindly toward a surface
flecked with thoughts, like mosquitos landing
on a pond of rational awareness . . . considerable pain . . .
eye slowly focusing . . . a world narrowed down to
one drop of colorless fluid falling
at the speed of light, but never arriving,
suspended forever . . . like a celestial
surface noise reverberating through all being . . .
the viewer should be made to feel as though
he or she is climbing individual vision strands
like shiny beanstalks . . . shinnying slick firehouse chrome poles
up from basal thinghood to a cool soul life
that floats above in transparent atmosphere . . .
out of body now . . . cool now . . . cool now . . .

Years later she finds herself upon the back of a long-maned,
        thick-hoofed pony
crossing the hellish terrain of the Kolgoz Depression
where subterranean fires, like quick darting tongues, lick her shoes
when she dismounts to inspect the reddish, crumbling earth . . .

she proceeds by caravan from Cochin to Korea to Zimbabwe . . .
rides a yak bearing sacks of gold through a blinding mountain
        blizzard in Nepal . . .
spends a night making love to a native chief in a tent at the brink
        of Mauna Loa . . .
gallops around the big island of Hawaii four times on horseback . . .
survives shipwreck on a storm battered schooner bound toward
        Puget Sound . . .

in Leadville falls into a liaison with a desperado, culminating in
        his going insane . . .
lives for two years among the hairy Ainu of Northern Japan . . .
witnesses the crucifixion of political criminals in China . . .
rides a mule up and down the trade routes of Turkey, Russia
        and Tibet . . .

acquires a farm to raise and breed marsupial mice in the bush
        of Tasmania . . .
bicycles through the Andes carrying only a spare tire, a Bible, a dagger,
and a cast-iron tea kettle strapped to the handlebars . . . bathes in milk
in the imperial court of Persia . . . is blown up by a landmine
        near Victoria Falls . . .
makes her way on foot from the mouth of the Nile to Bombay to Mongolia
via the great baked expanse of the Deccan plateau
where the sun beats down without mercy on a thin brown skin of grass
like a stick beating the back of a cowed and mangy dog . . .
scorns a Pullman to traverse Canada in winter by dog team . . .
at the end assumes the role of a *femme fatale* . . .
spends three years maddening all her lovers by staring into
        a champagne glass
and by the unmentionable precision of her desires . . . and leaves behind
in each of her lovers' minds an array of colors—whites, grays,
magentas, blacks, ochres, greens, and bronze-lustred blues . . . all later
reduced to sepia by newsreel clips of the day . . . inspires biographies . . .
has a movie written about her career as an adventuress,
        by Paul Morand . . .
Hecate et ses chiens . . . showing in terrible detail how one
male after another has been destroyed by her great beauty
and perversity . . . all for a whim . . . now she floats eighteen inches
above the cool aluminum repose of the operating table . . . tipping
        the surgeon's arm . . .
"Swab. Clamp. Retractor. Never mind. Looks like we lost this one . . ."

Crossing the border again . . . *into another life*

Some passages of this long poem appeared previously in: *Ink*, *Another Chicago Magazine*, *Conjunctions*, and *Dark As Day* (Smithereens Press).

This poem was handset in Ehrhardt and Forum Capitals by Denise Grimsman, designed and printed by David Duer on Strathmore Grandee text, and sewn into Grandee wrappers.

This is number **50** of an edition of 500, signed by the author and artist.